The Pocket Guide Of Golf Rules

Golf Rules Simplified

Anthony A. Blunden

Watchwood Publishing

While writing *The Pocket Guide Of Golf Rules*, I have received unlimited support from my wife, Barbara, my family and my friends. To each of them, I express my deepest appreciation. Also, I wish to acknowledge and thank Johnny Miller for his generosity and contributions to the game of golf.

Copyright © 2004
by Anthony A. Blunden
First Paperback Edition: 1994

Library of Congress Catalog 94-60710

ISBN 0-9641877-2-8

Watchwood Publishing
P.O. Box 1387
Orinda, CA 94563
(925) 253-1165

FORWARD

Most sports have rules which govern play. Golf is no exception.

The United States Golf Association and the Royal and Ancient Golf Club of St. Andrews jointly write the *Rules of Golf*, the rules which govern play throughout the world.

Since the majority of golfers wish to play by the rules, there has long been a need to have a handbook that instantly answers rules questions that arise during play. You will find that *The Pocket Guide Of Golf Rules* is that handbook! Authored by Tony Blunden, *The Pocket Guide Of Golf Rules* explains the rules in plain language, provides helpful diagrams, and includes humorous illustrations to benefit golfers of all abilities.

I enthusiastically recommend *The Pocket Guide Of Golf Rules* because I know it will provide you with quick answers to your rules questions and add to your enjoyment of the game of golf!

Johnny Miller

TABLE OF CONTENTS

STROKE PLAY AND MATCH PLAY

<u>Stroke Play And Match Play Defined:</u>
Stroke play, also sometimes known as medal play, is a competition based on the total number of strokes played. Match play is a competition based on the number of holes won. The typical penalty in stroke play is the loss of two strokes. The typical penalty in match play is the loss of the hole. The players in a stroke play competition are call competitors, or fellow-competitors if playing in your group. In a match play competition the player or side you are competing against is called your opponent.

You know, Barb...when we're competing in match play, we're called *opponents*.

Procedure When You're Unsure Of Your Rights-In Stroke Play Competition (Rule 3-3): In stroke play, if you become unsure of the proper way to proceed during play of a hole, continue play with your original ball using one alternative and also play a second ball from the point of uncertainty, using another alternative. Before playing either ball from the point of uncertainty, tell the marker or one of your fellow-competitors what you're going to do and with which ball you want to score if the rules will permit. You must inform the tournament committee before returning your score card that you played a second ball, and why or you will be disqualified. The committee will then determine your final score for that hole. Note that a second ball is not a provisional ball.

Procedure When You're Unsure Of Your Rights-In Match Play Competition (Rule 2-5): In match play, the playing of a second ball is not permitted. If you and your opponent cannot reach agreement as to how an uncertainty should be resolved, and no committee member is available within a reasonable time, you have the right to play the hole under protest if you believe your opponent is proceeding incorrectly. In order to preserve your right to present a claim to the tournament committee at the end of the round, you must tell your opponent

2

that you intend to make a claim at the end of the round, state the facts which you believe give rise to the claim and indicate that you want the Rules of Golf to be applied. This information must be stated to your opponent before either of you play from the teeing ground of the next hole, or, if it's the last hole, before you leave the putting green, otherwise the claim will not be considered by the tournament committee at the conclusion of the match.

Additional Pointers: (1) In match play, you are *dormie* when you are ahead by the same number of holes that remain to be played. (2) In match play, if you incur a penalty after you have holed out and your opponent is left with a stroke to tie the hole, the hole is tied. (3) In match play, you or your opponent may concede a stroke, a hole, or the match. Once a concession is given, it cannot be declined or withdrawn. (4) In match play, you may complete play of a hole even though your next stroke has been conceded. However, if your continued play assists your partner in a four-ball or best-ball match, your partner will be disqualified for the hole.

EQUIPMENT

Equipment Defined: Everything you use, wear and carry with you on the golf course is considered to be your equipment, except: (1) your ball marker(s) when being used to mark the position of a ball or an area in which a ball is to be dropped, and (2) your balls that are being played on the hole you are playing.

Procedure When Your Ball Hits Your Equipment (Rule 19-2): In stroke play, if you, your partner, either of your caddies, or any equipment of you or your partner accidentally stops or deflects your moving ball, after a stroke, you must play your ball where it comes to rest, with a two-stroke penalty. In match play, you will lose the hole.

Procedure Regarding Fourteen Club Limit (Rule 4-4): As part of your equipment, you are permitted to carry a maximum of fourteen clubs during your round. You may share clubs, but only with your partner, and only if you have no more than fourteen clubs in total between you. In stroke play, you will incur a two-stroke penalty for each hole played with more than fourteen clubs, with a maximum penalty of four strokes per round. In match play, the score of the match is adjusted after play is finished on the hole where the breach is discovered. One hole is then deducted from the score of the offending player's side for each hole played with more than fourteen clubs, with a maximum deduction of two holes per round.

Additional Pointers: (1) As soon as you discover that you're carrying more than fourteen clubs, announce which ones are extra and take them out of play. If you use the extra clubs during the remainder of the round, you will be disqualified. (2) You are not permitted to change clubs in the middle of a round. However, if a club becomes unfit in the normal course of play during a round, or if you start with less than fourteen clubs, you may replace or add the proper number of additional clubs. The additional clubs may not be borrowed from those clubs selected for play by another player who is playing on the course. (3) You are permitted to move your equipment out of the path of a moving ball, without penalty. Thus, if your clubs are on the surface of the putting green and your ball is moving toward them, your partner may move your clubs, without penalty, so they won't be struck by your moving ball. (4) A ball you are playing on the hole you are playing becomes your equipment when it has been lifted and has not yet been put back in play. (5) When you share a golf cart, the cart and everything in it are considered to be your equipment unless the cart is being moved by the player sharing the cart, in which case the moving cart and everything in it are considered to be the equipment of the other player.

TEEING GROUND

Teeing Ground Defined: The teeing ground is a rectangular area that is located at the start of each hole. The front and sides of the rectangular area are defined by imaginary lines that run along the outside portions of the tee-markers. The distance from the front line of the teeing ground to the back line of the teeing ground is two club-lengths. Your ball is within the teeing ground if any part of your ball is within this rectangular area.

Procedure For Playing From The Teeing Ground (Rules 11-4): In stroke play, your ball must be located within the teeing ground when you play your first stroke on each hole. If your ball is located outside the teeing ground when you play your first stroke, the strokes played with that ball are not counted. Instead, you must start over by playing another ball from within the teeing ground, with a two-stroke penalty. Thus you will be hitting three. Also, in stroke play, if you start play of a hole with a ball located outside the teeing ground, and then fail to correct your mistake before beginning play on the next hole, or, in the case of the final hole, if you leave the putting green before declaring your intention to correct your mistake on that hole, you will be disqualified. In match play, if your ball is located outside the teeing ground when you play your first stroke, there is no penalty. However, your opponent must either accept your shot or immediately require you to cancel the stroke, and instead have you replay a first stroke with a ball located within the teeing ground.

Additional Pointers: (1) You may stand outside the teeing ground to hit a ball located within it. (2) Your ball is *in play* as soon as you play a stroke from the teeing ground. (3) If you accidentally knock your ball off the tee before you have played a stroke on the hole, or if your ball falls off the tee before you have played a stroke on the hole, simply replace your ball, without penalty, since your ball is not yet in play. (4) If you play a first stroke from the teeing ground and miss your ball completely, your ball is in play. If you thereafter accidentally knock your ball off the tee or it falls off the tee before you begin your next stroke, you must replace it and take a one-stroke penalty for ball movement. (5) You will incur a two-stroke penalty in stroke play, and the loss of the hole in match play, if, before you play your first stroke with any ball from the teeing ground of the hole you are playing, you move a tee-marker in order to avoid interference with your stance, the area of your intended swing, or your line of play.

ORDER OF PLAY

Order Of Play Defined: The order of play sets forth the proper hitting rotation for the players in your group.

Procedure For Determining The Order Of Play From The Tee (Rule 10): Unless specified in advance, the order of play on the first teeing ground is usually decided by the toss of a coin or the flip of a tee. Thereafter, the player with the lowest score on the hole in stroke play, or the side that wins the hole in match play, has the honors and plays first on the next tee. The order of play on the next tee remains the same when there is a tie.

Procedure For Determining The Order Of Play During Play Of The Hole (Rule 10): After the tee shots have been played, the player farthest from the hole plays first. If two balls are equidistant from the hole, decide the order of play by the toss of a coin or the flip of a tee. When your original ball is not to be played as it lies and you are required to replay a stroke from where your previous stroke was played, the order of play is determined by the spot from which your previous stroke was made. When your original ball may be played from a place other than where your previous stroke was made, the order of play is determined by the position where your original ball came to rest.

Procedure If You Accidentally Play Out Of Turn (Rule 10): In stroke play, if you accidentally play out of turn, there is no penalty. Similarly, in match play, if you play a stroke when it's your opponent's turn, there is no penalty. However, in match play, your opponent may either accept your shot or immediately require you to cancel the stroke and instead have you replay the stroke when it's your turn.

Additional Pointers: (1) You will be playing out of turn if you play a provisional ball from the teeing ground before your fellow-competitor in stroke play, or opponent in match play, has played a first stroke. (2) In stroke play, you may be disqualified if you seek to gain an advantage by intentionally playing out of turn. (3) In a four-ball match, the side with a ball farthest from the hole may play either ball first. (4) In match play, if you play your first stroke on a hole from outside the teeing ground and your opponent requires you to cancel the stroke and play over, play your next stroke before your opponent plays.

PLAYING THE BALL AS IT LIES

<u>As It Lies Defined:</u> One of the basic principles in golf is that you should play the course as you find it and the ball as it lies, unless the rules allow otherwise. In other words, after you have played a stroke and your ball has come to rest, there should be no unauthorized modification of the lie of the ball, your line of play to the hole, or the area of your intended swing before you play your next stroke.

Procedure For Playing The Ball As It Lies
(Rule 13): It is a two-stroke penalty in stroke play, and a loss of the hole in match play, to:

1. *Improve your lie.* You are not permitted to use your foot, club, or anything else to press down grass, soil, sand or other irregularities that are behind or near your ball, except when your ball is on the teeing ground. When your ball is outside a sand bunker or water hazard and you are at address, you are permitted to set your clubhead on the ground behind your ball, but you may not press your clubhead into the ground.

2. *Improve your line of play.* You are not permitted to bend, break or remove anything that is fixed or growing in order to improve your line of play to the hole. However, you are permitted to remove movable obstructions on your line of play. You are also permitted to remove loose impediments on your line of play, as long as both your ball and the loose impediments are not in the same sand bunker or water hazard.

3. *Improve the area of your intended swing.* You are not permitted to bend, break, or remove anything that is fixed or growing in order to improve the area of your intended swing. Thus, if you improve the area of your intended swing by knocking down leaves, or even just one leaf, during your practice swing, you will be penalized. You will also

be penalized if you improve the area of your intended swing by wrapping branches around each other or by standing on them. Note: You are permitted to fairly take your stance and to reasonably make a stroke. In other words, there is no penalty if some branches bend or break while you are backing into a bush or tree in order to get in position to fairly play a stroke or if they bend or break while you are reasonably taking your backswing or downswing.

PLAYING FROM HAZARDS

Hazard Defined: A hazard is a sand bunker or a water hazard.

Remember, Molly...make sure you don't *ground your club* in the bunker!

Procedure For Playing From Sand Bunkers And Water Hazards (Rule 13): When your ball is in a sand bunker or a water hazard, it is a two-stroke penalty in stroke play, and a loss of hole in match play, to:

1. *Ground your club.* Your club may not touch the ground in a sand bunker, or the ground or water in a water hazard, when you take a practice swing or when you take your backswing during your actual swing. Your club may touch long grass and other vegetation in a water hazard when you are making a practice swing, or during the backswing of your actual swing, as long as you don't improve your lie or ground your club while doing so. You may ground your club in any grass-covered area which is around and within a sand bunker since the grass-covered portion is not considered to be part of the sand bunker. Note: There is no penalty if your club touches the ground or water in a hazard when you are attempting to prevent a fall.

2. *Move loose impediments.* You are permitted to touch and move loose impediments with your feet when approaching the ball in the hazard, provided you don't improve the lie of the ball or the area of your intended stance or swing. You are not permitted to touch or move loose impediments, such as leaves or twigs, that are in the sand bunker or water hazard where your ball is located, except when searching for a lost ball. Once you have located a ball in the sand bunker or water hazard, you are not permitted to remove additional loose impediments in

order to identify the owner of the ball since there is no penalty for playing a wrong ball from a sand bunker or a water hazard.

3. *Test the ground condition.* You are not permitted to test the ground condition of the hazard your ball is in or the ground condition of a similar hazard. You are permitted to set your extra clubs or the rake down in a sand bunker or water hazard, as long as you don't test the sand or soil by doing so. You are also permitted to smooth out the sand or soil after making a stroke in the sand bunker or water hazard, even if your ball is still in the hazard, as long as you don't improve your lie or get some benefit for subsequent play of the hole.

4. *Improve your lie.* You are not permitted to improve the lie of your ball. However, you are permitted to remove movable obstructions, such as movable water hazard stakes, bottles and rakes, even if your ball lies in the sand bunker or water hazard. If your ball moves as a result of removing the obstruction, replace your ball in its original location, without penalty.

5. *Delay a stroke.* You are not permitted to delay making a stroke to allow the wind or current to move your ball to a better spot in a water hazard.

Additional Pointers: (1) In both stroke play and match play, you will incur a one-stroke penalty if you touch or lift a ball to identify it when it is located in a sand bunker or a water hazard. (2) When your ball is in a sand bunker, you are entitled to casual water, unplayable lie, burrowing animal and immovable obstruction relief. You are not entitled to such relief when your ball is in a water hazard. Instead, you must proceed under the water hazard rules. (3) There is no embedded ball relief when your ball is in a sand bunker or a water hazard. (4) If, without realizing that you are breaking a rule, you take several practice swings in a sand bunker or water hazard before playing your ball, and touch the ground with your club each time, the penalty in stroke play is the loss of two strokes in total, not the loss of two strokes for each time you ground your club. (5) Normally, when your ball is in a bunker, you are not permitted to touch or move stones lying in or touching the bunker. However, if a committee determines that the stones in the bunkers could be a danger to players and interfere with the proper playing of the game, a local rule may be adopted stating that such stones may be treated as movable obstructions.

RELIEF FROM LOOSE IMPEDIMENTS

Loose Impediments Defined: Loose impediments are objects made by nature, while obstructions are objects made by man. By definition, loose impediments cannot be (1) growing, (2) fixed to something, (3) solidly embedded, or (4) adhering to the ball. Examples of loose impediments are leaves, loose stones, aeration plugs, cut grass, and twigs. Worms and insects, and casts or heaps made by them, are considered to be loose impediments, but the dew on the grass is not. Sand and loose soil are loose impediments only when they are on the putting green. Snow and natural ice may be treated as either casual water or loose impediments. Artificial ice is an obstruction rather than a loose impediment.

Procedure For Relief From Loose Impediments (Rule 23-1): If your ball is at rest, you are permitted to remove loose impediments such as twigs and leaves, without penalty, unless both your ball and the loose impediments lie in or touch the same sand bunker or water hazard. If your ball is off the putting green and moves to another spot as a direct result of removing loose impediments, replace your ball, with a one-stroke penalty. If you remove loose impediments when both your ball and the loose impediments lie in the same sand bunker or water hazard, you will incur a two-stroke penalty in stroke play, and the loss of the hole in match play, unless the removal occurs while searching for your ball in the hazard. Note, however, that when both your ball and the loose impediments are in a sand bunker or water hazard, you are permitted to touch and move the loose impediments with your feet when approaching your ball, provided you don't improve the lie of your ball or the area of your intended stance or swing.

Additional Pointers: (1) Sand and loose soil are loose impediments only when they are on the putting green. Thus, you will incur a two-stroke penalty in stroke play, and the loss of the hole in match play, if you remove sand or loose soil from the apron or from some other location through the green. (2) You will incur a two-stroke penalty in stroke play, and the loss of the hole in match play, if, while a ball is in motion, you remove a loose impediment that might influence the movement of the ball. (3) Pebbles located in sand bunkers are usually considered to be loose impediments. Thus, when your ball is in a sand bunker you are not permitted to touch or remove pebbles lying in or touching the same bunker. However, if a committee determines that the pebbles could be a danger to players and interfere with play, a local rule may be adopted stating that the pebbles may be treated as movable obstructions. (4) If your ball is lost in a sand bunker or water hazard and covered by loose impediments or sand, you are permitted to remove as many loose impediments or as much sand as is necessary to see part of *a* ball.

EMBEDDED BALL RELIEF

Embedded Ball Defined: When a ball is plugged in its own pitch-mark, with part of the ball below the level of the ground, it is an embedded ball. The ball does not have to touch bare ground in order to be considered embedded. A pitch-mark is a hole in the ground that is made by the impact of a ball.

Procedure For Relief When Your Ball Is Embedded-Outside A Sand Bunker And Outside A Water Hazard (Rule 25-2): When you have an embedded ball in the fairway or any closely mown area of the course, and not in a sand bunker or water hazard, you may:

    1. Play your ball as it lies, without penalty; or

    2. Lift, clean, and then drop your ball, without penalty, as close as possible to the pitch-mark, no nearer the hole.

    Note: All portions of the course, including paths through the rough, are considered closely mown areas when they are cut to the same height as a fairway, or less.

Procedure For Relief When Your Ball Is Embedded-In A Sand Bunker Or A Water Hazard (Rule 25-2): When you have an embedded ball in a sand bunker, there is no embedded ball relief, and thus you must either play the ball as it lies or declare your ball unplayable and proceed under the rules for an unplayable lie.   When you have an embedded ball in a water hazard, there is no embedded ball or unplayable lie relief, and thus you must proceed under the water hazard rules.

    Additional Pointers: (1) If your ball is embedded off the putting green, you are not allowed to repair your pitch-mark before dropping your ball. However, if you drop your ball and it rolls into the pitch-mark, you must re-drop it, without penalty. (2) If your ball is embedded on the putting green, you may mark, lift and clean your ball, repair the pitch-mark and then replace your ball, without penalty. (3) When your ball is located outside a sand bunker or water hazard, you may lift your ball, without penalty, to determine if it is embedded. Before lifting your ball, make sure you advise a fellow-competitor or marker in stroke play, or an opponent in match play, of your intention to lift it, give them an opportunity to watch, and then mark your ball before lifting it. (4) You may clean your ball when you take relief from an embedded ball. (5) If your ball becomes embedded when you drop it pursuant to an applicable rule, you may re-drop it. If it becomes embedded when re-dropped, place your ball as close as possible to the spot where the ball embedded on the re-drop, no nearer the hole. (6) A local rule may be adopted which permits relief when a ball is embedded through the green, even though it is not in a closely mown area.

LOST BALL (PENALTY)

This section is *not* applicable to:

    1. A ball lost in a water hazard. See Water Hazard Options, page 38; or

    2. A ball lost in casual water, in ground under repair, a burrowing animal disturbance, or in an immovable obstruction. See Lost Ball (No Penalty), page 30.

Lost Ball Defined (Rule 27): Your original ball will be a lost ball if:

1. You can't find or identify your original ball within five minutes after your side or your side's caddies begin searching for it; or

2. You make a stroke at a substituted ball, even if you haven't searched for your original ball for the full five minutes, or at all; or

3. You play your provisional ball from a place where the original ball is likely to be or from a spot that is closer to the hole than that place.

Procedure When You Have A Lost Ball-Outside A Water Hazard (Rule 27): The penalty for a lost ball, in both stroke play and match play, is the loss of one stroke and distance. Thus, when your original ball is lost, you must drop another ball as close as possible to the spot where you last hit your original ball, no nearer the hole. For example, if you can't find your original ball after hitting your second shot, you must drop and hit another ball from where you hit your second shot, but instead of hitting three you will be hitting four since your third stroke is a penalty stroke. If your original ball was teed and hit from the teeing ground, you may tee and hit another ball from anywhere within the teeing ground.

Procedure For Playing A Provisional Ball

(Rule 27): When there is a reasonable possibility that your original ball is lost outside a water hazard or is out of bounds, you may play a provisional ball to save time. The provisional ball must be played before you and your partner leave the hitting area and before your side begins searching for your original ball. Before playing a provisional ball, you must specifically announce that you are going to play a provisional ball. Then, when it's your turn to play, drop your provisional ball as close as possible to the spot where you last played your original ball, no nearer the hole. If you last played your original ball from the teeing ground, you may tee and play your provisional ball from anywhere within the teeing ground. You may continue to play the provisional ball until you reach the place where your original ball is likely to be. Then, if you find your original ball in bounds, pick up the provisional ball and continue play with your original ball, without penalty. However, if you are unable to find your original ball, continue play with the provisional ball, making it your ball in play, with a penalty of one stroke and distance. Once your provisional ball becomes the ball in play, you must continue to play the hole with it, even if you later find your original ball.

Since that might be a lost ball, you may want to hit a *provisional ball*, Molly!

Additional Pointers: (1) You are not required to search for a lost ball for a full five minutes, or for any time at all, before putting another ball in play. However, if you find your original ball in bounds before the five minute period has expired and before you make a stroke at a substituted ball, the original ball remains your ball in play, even if it's in an undesirable location, and even if you have orally declared it to be lost. (2) Always put an identification mark on your ball so you can identify the ball as yours, if found. (3) If your ball is lost in a water hazard, proceed under the water hazard rules rather than the rules for a lost ball.

LOST BALL (NO PENALTY)

Lost Ball (No Penalty) Defined: You have a lost ball that is applicable to this section if there is reasonable evidence to indicate that your ball is lost, in bounds, in one of the following four problem areas:

1. Casual water
2. Ground under repair
3. A burrowing animal disturbance
4. An immovable obstruction

Well, John...at least you won't be penalized this time for a *lost ball*!

Procedure When Your Ball Is Lost In One Of The Four Problem Areas-Outside A Sand Bunker, Outside A Water Hazard, And Not On A Putting Green (Rules 24 & 25): Determine the spot where your ball last entered the problem area. Next, determine the nearest point of relief (see page 50) from this spot that is not in a sand bunker, a water hazard or on a putting green. Drop your ball, without penalty, within one club-length of, and not nearer the hole than, your nearest point of relief, on a part of the course where there is no interference caused by the problem area and is not in a sand bunker, a water hazard, or on a putting green.

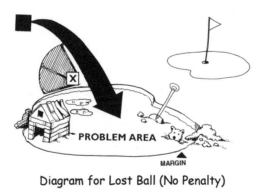

Diagram for Lost Ball (No Penalty)

Procedure When Your Ball Is Lost In One Of The Four Problem Areas-In A Sand Bunker (Rules 24 & 25):

1. Determine the spot where your ball last entered the problem area in the sand bunker. Next, determine the nearest point of relief (see page 50) from this spot in the sand bunker. Drop your ball, without penalty, in the sand bunker, within one club-length of, and not nearer the hole than, your nearest point of relief, where there is no interference caused by the problem area. Note: If complete relief is not possible when your ball is lost in ground under repair, casual water, or in a burrowing animal disturbance, drop your ball, without penalty, in the sand bunker, as near as possible to, and not nearer the hole than, where your ball last entered the problem area, in that part of the sand bunker which provides maximum available relief from the problem area; or

2. Determine the spot where your ball last entered the problem area in the sand bunker. Imagine a straight line that goes from the hole to that spot. Continue to extend the line straight back from that spot and then drop your ball, with a one-stroke penalty, behind the sand bunker and on the extended line, going as far back on the course as you want.

Procedure When Your Ball Is Lost In One Of The Four Problem Areas-On The Putting Green (Rules 24 & 25): Determine the nearest point of relief (see page 50) which is not in a sand bunker or water hazard. Place a substituted ball, without penalty, at this nearest point of relief. If complete relief is not possible, place your ball, without penalty, at the spot nearest to where your original ball entered the problem area, on ground that gives maximum available relief from the condition and is not in a sand bunker or water hazard. Note that the location of the nearest point of relief or the maximum available relief may be off the putting green.

Additional Pointers: (1) If your ball becomes lost in a *movable* obstruction, drop your ball, or place it if on the putting green, without penalty, as near as possible to the spot where your ball last entered the movable obstruction, no nearer the hole. (2) If your ball is lost in a water hazard, there is no relief, without penalty, from a burrowing animal disturbance, ground under repair, or an immovable obstruction that is located in the water hazard. Instead, you must proceed under the water hazard rules. (3) If you decide your original ball is lost and put another ball in play, you may not later play your original ball if you find it in bounds.

OUT OF BOUNDS

Out Of Bounds Defined: Your ball is out of bounds, and therefore out of play, when it comes to rest beyond markers that define the boundaries of the course. Out of bounds markers are often white stakes, white lines, fence posts, walls, railings and roads. When the boundary markers are stakes or fence posts, the out of bounds line runs along the nearest inside points, e.g. the golf course side rather than the out of bounds side of the stakes or posts, at ground level. When the boundary is defined by a line on the ground, the line itself is out of bounds. Your ball is in bounds unless all of it lies out of bounds.

Procedure When Your Ball Is Out Of Bounds (Rule 27): The penalty for hitting a ball out of bounds, in both stroke play and match play, is the loss of one-stroke and distance. When you hit a ball out of bounds, you must drop another ball as close as possible to the spot where you last hit, no nearer the hole. For example, if you hit your ball out of bounds on your third shot, you must drop and hit another ball from where you hit your third shot, but instead of hitting four you will be hitting five since your fourth stroke is a penalty stroke. If your original ball was hit from the teeing ground, you may tee and hit another ball from anywhere within the teeing ground.

I know my ball is not *out of bounds* as long as any part of it is in bounds!

Procedure For Playing A Provisional Ball (Rule 27): When there is a reasonable possibility that your original ball is out of bounds or is lost outside a water hazard, you may play a provisional ball to save time. The provisional ball must be played before you and your partner leave the hitting area and before your side begins searching for your original ball. Before playing a provisional ball, you must specifically announce that you are going to play a provisional ball. Then, when it's your turn to play, drop your provisional ball as close as possible to the spot where you last played your original ball, no nearer the hole. If you last played your original ball from the teeing ground, you may tee and play your provisional ball from anywhere within the teeing ground. You may continue to play the provisional ball until you reach the place where your original ball is likely to be. Then, if you discover that your original ball is in bounds, pick up the provisional ball and continue play with your original ball, without penalty. However, if you discover that your original ball is out of bounds, or is a lost ball, continue play

There's a penalty for removing the out of bounds marker, John!

with the provisional ball, making it your ball in play, with a penalty of one stroke and distance. Once your provisional ball becomes the ball in play, you must continue to play the hole with it, even if you later find that your original ball is in bounds.

Additional Pointers: (1) If an out of bounds marker for the hole you are playing interferes with your stance or swing when your ball is in bounds, you either have to play your ball as it lies or declare an unplayable lie. (2) If you remove an out of bounds marker to improve the area of your stance, swing, or line of play, you will incur a two-stroke penalty in stroke play, and the loss of the hole in match play, even if you replace it before making a stroke. (3) You may stand out of bounds to play a ball that is located in bounds. (4) An angled support of a boundary fence that is in bounds is an obstruction, but a concrete base of a boundary fence post below ground is not.

WATER HAZARD OPTIONS

Water Hazard Defined: If your ball is in a lake, pond, river, ditch or surface drainage ditch, it is in a water hazard, even if it is not in water. Water hazards are either *regular* water hazards, usually known simply as water hazards, or *lateral* water hazards. Regular water hazards are defined by yellow stakes or lines and usually have three options of play. Lateral water hazards are defined by red stakes or lines and usually have five options of play. The stakes and lines which are used as markers to define the margins of the water hazard are themselves part of the water hazard. Your ball is in the water hazard if it lies in, or any part of it touches, the water hazard.

Say, John...why don't you take *water hazard relief*?

Procedure When Your Ball Lies In, Or Is Lost In, A Regular Water Hazard (Rule 26):

1. Play your ball as it lies, without penalty; or

2. Drop a ball, with a one-stroke penalty, as close as possible to the spot where you last played a stroke, no nearer the hole. Note that if you last played from the teeing ground, you may re-tee your ball; or

3. Determine the spot where your ball last crossed the margin of the water hazard. Imagine a straight line that goes from the hole to that spot. Continue to extend the line straight back from that spot and then drop your ball, with a one-stroke penalty, behind the water hazard and on the extended line, going as far back on the course as you want.

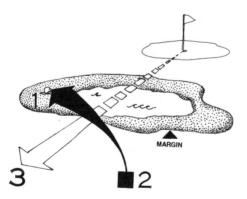

Diagram for "Regular" Water Hazard Options

Procedure When Your Ball Lies In, Or Is Lost In, A Lateral Water Hazard (Rule 26):

1. Play your ball as it lies, without penalty; or

2. Drop a ball, with a one-stroke penalty, as close as possible to the spot where you last played a stroke, no nearer the hole. Note that if you last played from the teeing ground, you may re-tee your ball; or

3. Determine the spot where your ball last crossed the margin of the water hazard. Imagine a straight line that goes from the hole to that spot. Continue to extend the line straight back from that spot and then drop your ball, with a one-stroke penalty, behind the water hazard and on the extended line, going as far back on the course as you want; or

4. Drop a ball, with a one-stroke penalty, outside the lateral water hazard and within two club-lengths of where your ball last crossed the margin of the lateral water hazard, no nearer the hole; or

5. Drop a ball, with a one-stroke penalty, on the opposite side of the lateral water hazard. Determine the distance from the hole to the spot where your ball last crossed the margin of the lateral water hazard. Next, find a spot on the margin on the other side of the lateral water hazard that is equidistant from the hole. Finally, drop your ball outside the lateral water hazard, within two club-lengths of this new spot, no nearer the hole.

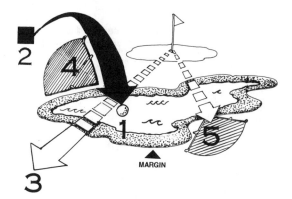

Diagram for Lateral Water Hazard Options

Procedure For Playing From Drop Areas (Appendix 1): If a drop area is provided as an additional option of play, you may drop your ball, with a one-stroke penalty, anywhere within the drop area. If your ball rolls out of the drop area and comes to rest nearer the hole but within two club-lengths of where it first hit the ground in the drop area, it will be in play as long as it is not in a sand bunker, a water hazard, or on a putting green, and as long as it is not closer to the hole than where the ball last crossed the margin of the water hazard or lateral water hazard.

Procedure Regarding Play Of A Provisional Ball When Your Original Ball Is In A Water Hazard (Rule 27):

Unless there is a local rule to the contrary, you may play a provisional ball only when there is a reasonable possibility that your original ball is lost outside a water hazard or is out of bounds. If you know that your original ball is in a water hazard, you are not permitted to play a provisional ball. If you do play a provisional ball when your original ball is definitely in the water hazard, your original ball will be considered a lost ball and the provisional ball will become your ball in play, with a penalty of one stroke and distance.

Procedure When A Ball Played From Within A Water Hazard Becomes Lost Outside A Water Hazard Or Goes Out Of Bounds (Rule 26-2):

You will incur a one-stroke penalty if, as a result of playing a stroke from a water hazard, your ball becomes lost outside a water hazard or goes out of bounds. Your options of play are then as follows:

1. Drop a ball, without any additional penalty, as close as possible, and no nearer the hole, to where your ball was located when you last played a stroke in the water hazard; or

2. Determine the spot where your original ball last crossed the margin of the water hazard. Imagine a straight line that goes from the hole to that spot. Continue to extend the line straight back from that spot and then drop a ball, with an additional one-stroke penalty, behind the water hazard and on the extended line, going as far back on the course as you want; or

3. If your ball last crossed the margin of a lateral water hazard, you may proceed, with an additional one-stroke penalty, using either procedure number 4 or procedure number 5 on page 40; or

4. Play a ball, with an additional one-stroke penalty, as close as possible to where your ball was located when you last played if from outside the water hazard.

Procedure When A Ball Played From Within A Water Hazard Remains in The Water Hazard (Rule 26-2): If you play your ball from a water hazard and it stays in the water hazard, your options of play are then the following:

1. Proceed using options 1-3 on page 39 or, if applicable, options 1-5 on page 40; or

2. Play a ball, with a one-stroke penalty, as close as possible to where your ball was located when you last played it from outside the water hazard.

Note: If you select option 2 on page 39 and then decide not to play your dropped ball, you may, by adding an additional penalty stroke, proceed under options 3, 4 (if applicable), or 5 (if applicable) on page 40, or, under option 2 above.

Additional Pointers: (1) If you lose your ball, you must proceed under the rules relating to a ball lost outside of the water hazard unless there is reasonable evidence to indicate that your ball is actually lost in the water hazard. (2) If a movable water hazard stake interferes with your ball, stance or swing, you may remove the stake, without penalty, even if your ball is in the water hazard. If the water hazard stake is immovable and interferes with your ball, stance or swing, you are entitled to immovable obstruction relief if your ball is located outside the water hazard. If the water hazard stake is immovable and your ball is located in the water hazard, you are not entitled to immovable obstruction relief. Instead, you must proceed under the water hazard rules. (3) If your ball is in a water hazard, there is no embedded ball, unplayable lie, burrowing animal, ground under repair, or immovable obstruction relief. Instead you must proceed under the water hazard rules. (4) When you are permitted to lift your ball in a water hazard, you may clean it before dropping it. (5) You may be prohibited, by local rule, from playing your ball from a water hazard when the water hazard is in an environmentally-sensitive area. (6) To properly play your ball from a water hazard, refer to the section entitled Playing From Hazards, page 16.

UNPLAYABLE LIES

Unplayable Lie Defined: If you are unable to play your ball, or if for any reason you simply choose not to play it from its present location, you may declare it *unplayable*, except when your ball is in a water hazard.

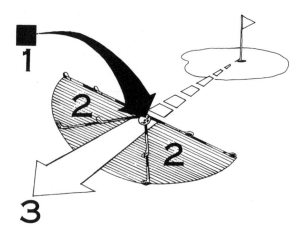

Diagram for Unplayable Lie Options

Procedure For Relief From An Unplayable Lie-When Your Ball Is Outside A Sand Bunker and Outside A Water Hazard And Not On A Putting Green (Rule 28):

1. Drop your ball, with a one-stroke penalty, as close as possible to the spot where you last played a stroke, no nearer the hole. If you last played a stroke from the putting green, place your ball. If you last played a stroke from the teeing ground, drop or re-tee your ball anywhere within the teeing ground; or

2. Drop your ball, with a one-stroke penalty, within two club-lengths of where your ball is located, no nearer the hole; or

3. Imagine a straight line that goes from the hole to where your ball is located in the unplayable lie. Continue to extend the line straight back from where your ball is located and then drop your ball on the extended line, with a one-stroke penalty, going as far back on the course as you want.

Procedure For Relief From An Unplayable Lie-When Your Ball Is In A Sand Bunker (Rule 28):

1. Drop your ball, with a one-stroke penalty, as close as possible to the spot where you last played a stroke, no nearer the hole; or

2. Drop your ball in the sand bunker, with a one-stroke penalty, within two club-lengths of where your ball is located, no nearer the hole; or

3. Imagine a straight line that goes from the hole to where your ball is located in the unplayable lie. Continue to extend the line straight back from where your ball is located and then drop your ball on that extended line, with a one-stroke penalty, going as far back as you want, but staying within the sand bunker.

Procedure For Relief From An Unplayable Lie-When Your Ball Is Above The Ground (Rule 28): If your ball comes to rest above the ground, in a bush or tree for example, and you elect to take relief for an unplayable lie, first determine a spot on the ground that is directly below your ball. Then proceed with the appropriate relief from that spot on the ground.

Additional Pointers: (1) Take care when you drop your ball since you are not always entitled to a re-drop, without penalty. For example, if you take a drop from an unplayable lie and your ball rolls less than two club-lengths, no nearer the hole, and back into the original unplayable lie, you are not allowed to re-drop it without penalty. Instead you must play the ball as it lies or proceed, once again, under the rules for an unplayable lie. (2) If your ball is in a water hazard, there is no unplayable lie relief. Instead you must proceed under the water hazard rules. (3) You may clean your ball whenever it is lifted from an unplayable lie. (4) You may use any club in your bag to measure two club-lengths from the location of your ball. (5) When you declare your ball unplayable through the green, you may drop your ball in a hazard.

NEAREST POINT OF RELIEF

Nearest Point Of Relief Defined: The nearest point of relief is a spot on the course that, once determined, eliminates interference with your ball, stance or the area of your intended swing caused by one of the following conditions:

    (1) An immovable obstruction

    (2) Casual water

    (3) Ground under repair

    (4) A burrowing animal disturbance

Procedure For Determining The Nearest Point Of Relief: First, determine what club, address position, direction of play and swing (right or left-handed) you would have used for your next stroke if there had been no interference. The nearest point of relief is then the spot on the course that:

    (1) Is nearest to where your ball lies (or, if your ball is lost, nearest to where your ball last entered the condition); and

    (2) Is not nearer the hole than where your ball lies (or, if your ball is lost, not nearer the hole than where your ball last entered the condition); and

    (3) Is free of interference caused by the condition when using the same club, address position, direction of play and swing (right or left-handed).

RELIEF FROM BURROWING ANIMAL DISTURBANCES

<u>Burrowing Animals Defined:</u> Some reptiles, some birds and some animals live in holes they make in the ground. Collectively these creatures are referred to as burrowing animals and include moles, rabbits, gophers, and salamanders. A hole, a cast (such as the hill made by a mole), or a runway made by a burrowing animal is referred to as a burrowing animal disturbance.

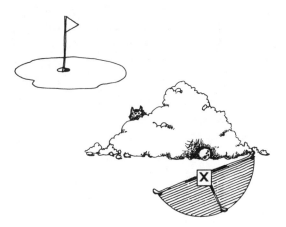

Diagram for Burrowing Animal Relief

Procedure For Relief-Generally (Rule 25-1): You are entitled to relief if your ball lies in or touches a burrowing animal disturbance or if a burrowing animal disturbance interferes with your stance or the area of your intended swing, or line of putt when your ball is on the putting green. There is no such relief when there is interference caused by a non-burrowing animal such as a dog, a deer, or a raccoon, unless so marked. If your ball becomes lost in a burrowing animal disturbance, see Lost Ball (No Penalty), page 30.

Procedure For Relief From Interference Caused By A Burrowing Animal Disturbance-Outside A Sand Bunker And Outside A Water Hazard And Not On A Putting Green (Rule 25-1)): Determine the spot known as the nearest point of relief (see page 50) that is not in a sand bunker, a water hazard or on a putting green. Drop your ball, without penalty, within one club-length of, and not nearer the hole than, this nearest point of relief, on a part of the course free from the interference caused by the disturbance and not in a sand bunker, a water hazard, or on a putting green.

Procedure For Relief From Interference Caused By A Burrowing Animal Disturbance In A Sand Bunker (Rule 25-1):

1. Determine a spot in the sand bunker that is the nearest point of relief (see page 50). Drop your ball in the sand bunker, without penalty, within one club-length of, and not nearer the hole than, this nearest point of relief, where there is no interference caused by the disturbance. Note: If complete relief from the disturbance is not possible, drop your ball, without penalty, in the sand bunker as near as possible to, and not nearer the hole than, where your ball was originally at rest, in that part of the sand bunker which provides maximum available relief from the disturbance; or

2. Imagine a straight line that goes from the hole to the spot where your ball came to rest in the sand bunker. Continue to extend the line straight back from that spot and then drop your ball, with a one-stroke penalty, behind the sand bunker and on the extended line, going as far back on the course as you want.

Procedure For Relief From Interference Caused By A Burrowing Animal Disturbance-When Your Ball Is On The Putting Green (Rule 25-1): Determine the spot known as the nearest point of relief (see page 50) that is not in a sand bunker or

water hazard. Lift your ball and place it, without penalty, at this nearest point of relief. If complete relief is not possible, place your ball, without penalty, at the spot nearest to where it lay, which gives maximum available relief from the disturbance and is not in a sand bunker or water hazard. Note that the location of the nearest point of relief or the maximum available relief may be off the putting green.

Additional Pointers: (1) You are not entitled to relief from a burrowing animal disturbance if you have to use an unnecessarily abnormal stance, swing, or direction of play before there is interference, or if the ball is clearly unplayable because of interference by something from which free relief is not available, such as a tree. (2) Your ball must be on the putting green in order to get relief from a burrowing animal disturbance that is on your line of putt on the putting green. (3) If your ball is in a water hazard, there is no relief from a burrowing animal disturbance. Instead you must proceed under the water hazard rules.

RELIEF FROM CASUAL WATER

Casual Water Defined: Casual water is a temporary accumulation of water that is anywhere on the course, except in a water hazard. It must be visible before or after you take your stance. In practice, if you see water accumulate around the soles of your shoes while taking your stance, you are in casual water. Snow and natural ice may be treated as either casual water or loose impediments. Dew and frost are not considered casual water.

Diagram for Casual Water Relief

Procedure For Relief-Generally: You are entitled to relief if your ball lies in or touches casual water or if casual water interferes with your stance or the area of your intended swing, or line of putt when your ball is on the putting green. If your ball becomes lost in casual water, see Lost Ball (No Penalty), page 30.

Procedure For Relief From Interference Caused By Casual Water-Outside A Sand Bunker And Outside A Water Hazard And Not On A Putting Green (Rule 25-1): Determine the spot known as the nearest point of relief (see page 50) that is not in a sand bunker, a water hazard or on a putting green. Drop your ball, without penalty, within one club-length of, and not nearer the hole than, this nearest point of relief, on a part of the course free from the interference caused by the disturbance and not in a sand bunker, a water hazard, or on a putting green.

Procedure For Relief From Interference Caused By Casual Water-In A Sand Bunker (Rule 25-1):
1. Determine a spot in the sand bunker that is the nearest point of relief (see page 50). Drop your ball in the sand bunker, without penalty, within one club-length of, and not nearer the hole than, this

nearest point of relief, where there is no interference caused by the disturbance. Note: If complete relief from the disturbance is not possible, drop your ball, without penalty, in the sand bunker as near as possible to, and not nearer the hole than, where your ball was originally at rest, in that part of the sand bunker which provides maximum available relief from the disturbance; or

2. Imagine a straight line that goes from the hole to the spot where your ball came to rest in the sand bunker. Continue to extend the line straight back from that spot and then drop your ball, with a one-stroke penalty, behind the sand bunker and on the extended line, going as far back on the course as you want.

Procedure For Relief From Interference Caused By Casual Water On The Putting Green-When Your Ball Is On The Putting Green (Rule 25-1): Determine the spot known as the nearest point of relief (see page 50) that is not in a sand bunker or water hazard. Lift your ball and place it, without penalty, at this nearest point of relief. If complete relief is not possible, place your ball, without penalty, at the spot nearest to where it lay, which gives maximum available relief from the disturbance and is not in a sand bunker or water hazard. Note that the location of the nearest point of relief or the maximum available relief may be off the putting green.

Additional Pointers: (1) You are not entitled to relief from interference caused by casual water if you have to use an unnecessarily abnormal stance, swing or direction of play before there is interference, or if the ball is clearly unplayable because of interference by something from which free relief is not available, such as a tree. (2) Your ball must be on the putting green in order to get relief from casual water that is on your line of putt on the putting green. (3) Since dew is not casual water or a loose impediment, you will incur a two-stroke penalty in stroke play, and a loss of the hole in match play, if you brush aside dew that is on your line of putt on the putting green. (4) If you find your ball in a sand bunker that is completely covered by casual water, you may proceed by using one of the options mentioned above, or you may proceed under the rules for an unplayable lie. (5) You are not entitled to casual water relief when your ball is in soft, mushy earth unless water is visible on the surface before or after you take your stance.

RELIEF FROM GROUND UNDER REPAIR

Ground Under Repair Defined: Ground under repair is that part of the course where play is discouraged or prohibited due to the conditions existing at that location. Ground under repair is usually marked as such, but also includes material that has been piled for removal and a hole made by a greenkeeper, even if not marked. However, unmarked areas containing grass cuttings, miscellaneous clippings, and other materials that are not intended to be removed and that have been left and abandoned on the course are not ground under repair. Similarly, bare patches, shallow ruts or grooves made by maintenance vehicles and aeration holes made by a greenkeeper are not ground under repair, unless so marked.

Procedure For Relief-Generally (Rule 25-1): You are entitled to relief if your ball lies in or touches ground under repair or if ground under repair interferes with your stance or the area of your intended swing, or line of putt when your ball is on the putting green. If your ball becomes lost in ground under repair, see Lost Ball (No Penalty), page 30.

59

Procedure For Relief From Interference Caused By Ground Under Repair-Outside A Sand Bunker And Outside A Water Hazard And Not On A Putting Green (Rule 25-1): Determine the spot known as the nearest point of relief (see page 50) that is not in a sand bunker, a water hazard or on a putting green. Drop your ball, without penalty, within one club-length of, and not nearer the hole than, this nearest point of relief, on a part of the course free from the interference caused by the disturbance and not in a sand bunker, a water hazard, or on a putting green.

Procedure For Relief From Interference Caused By Ground Under Repair-In A Sand Bunker (Rule 25-1):

1. Determine a spot in the sand bunker that is the nearest point of relief (see page 50). Drop your ball in the sand bunker, without penalty, within one club-length of, and not nearer the hole than, this nearest point of relief, where there is no interference caused by the disturbance. Note: If complete relief from the disturbance is not possible, drop your ball, without penalty, in the sand bunker as near as possible to, and not nearer the hole than, where your ball was originally at rest, in that part of the sand bunker which provides maximum available relief from the disturbance; or

2. Imagine a straight line that goes from the hole to the spot where your ball came to rest in the sand bunker. Continue to extend the line straight back from that spot and then drop your ball, with a one-stroke penalty, behind the sand bunker and on the extended line, going as far back on the course as you want.

Diagram for Ground Under Repair Relief

Procedure For Relief From Interference Caused By Ground Under Repair On The Putting Green-When Your Ball Is On The Putting Green (Rule 25-1):

Determine the spot known as the nearest point of relief (see page 50) that is not in a sand bunker or water hazard. Lift your ball and place it, without penalty, at this nearest point of relief. If complete relief is not possible, place your ball, without penalty, at the spot nearest to where it lay, which gives maximum available relief from the disturbance and is not in a sand bunker or water hazard. Note that the location of the nearest point of relief or the maximum available relief may be off the putting green.

Additional Pointers: (1) You are not entitled to relief from interference caused by ground under repair if you have to use an unnecessarily abnormal stance, swing or direction of play before there is interference, or if the ball is clearly unplayable because of interference by something from which free relief is not available, such as a tree. (2) Your ball must be on the putting green in order to get relief from ground under repair that is on your line of putt on the putting green. (3) If your ball is in a water hazard, there is no relief from ground under repair. Instead you must proceed under the water hazard rules.

RELIEF FROM OBSTRUCTIONS

Obstructions Defined: All man-made objects, including roads and paths made of artificial materials, are considered obstructions, except: (1) objects which are used to define out of bounds boundaries, such as stakes, walls, fences and railings, (2) construction which is deemed by the golf committee to be an integral part of the course, and (3) parts of immovable artificial objects which are themselves out of bounds. Obstructions are either movable or immovable. Movable obstructions can be lifted and moved without unreasonable effort, without unduly delaying play, and without damaging the course and include rakes, tin cans, movable water hazard stakes, and hoses. Immovable obstructions, such as cart paths, immovable water hazard stakes, and sprinkler heads, are fixed in place and obviously cannot be moved.

Procedure For Relief-Generally (Rule 24-1): When your ball is at rest, you may obtain relief from a movable obstruction by moving the obstruction. When your ball is at rest, you may obtain relief from an immovable obstruction by moving your ball. Note, however, that you are entitled to immovable obstruction relief only when your ball lies in or on the immovable obstruction, or when your ball lies so close to the immovable obstruction that it interferes with your stance, the area of your intended swing, or your line of putt when your ball is on the putting green.

Procedure For Relief From A Movable Obstruction-When Your Ball Isn't In Or On The Obstruction (Rule 24-1): If you wish to obtain relief from a movable obstruction simply remove the obstruction, without penalty. If your ball moves as a direct result of removing the movable obstruction,

Okay now, Molly. You may remove the can from the hazard, without penalty, because the can is an *obstruction.*

replace your ball, without penalty. This relief is available even when your ball is in a hazard.

Procedure For Relief From A Movable Obstruction-When Your Ball Lies In Or On The Obstruction (Rule 24-1): If your ball lies in or on a movable obstruction, such as a paper bag, lift the ball, remove the obstruction, and then drop your ball, or place your ball if it is on the putting green, without penalty, as close as possible to where the ball was at rest, no nearer the hole. This relief is available even when your ball is in a hazard.

Procedure For Relief From Interference Caused By An Immovable Obstruction-When Your Ball Is Outside A Sand Bunker And Outside A Water Hazard And Not On A Putting Green (24-2): If your ball lies in or on an immovable obstruction, or your ball lies so close to an immovable obstruction that it interferes with your stance or the area of your intended swing, you are entitled to immovable obstruction relief. Determine the spot known as the nearest point of relief (see page 50) that is not in a sand bunker, a water hazard or on a putting green. Drop your ball, without penalty, within one club-length of, and not nearer the hole than, this nearest point of relief, on a part of the course free from the interference caused by the immovable obstruction and not in a sand bunker, a water hazard, or on a putting green.

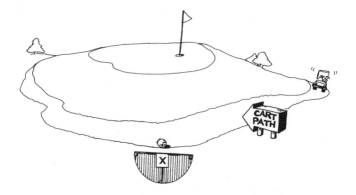

Diagram for Immovable Obstruction Relief

Procedure For Relief From Interference Caused By An Immovable Obstruction-When Your Ball Is In A Sand Bunker (Rule 24-2):

(1) Determine a spot in the sand bunker that is the nearest point of relief (see page 50). Drop your ball in the sand bunker, without penalty, within one club-length of, and not nearer the hole than, this nearest point of relief, where there is no interference caused by the immovable obstruction; or

2. Imagine a straight line that goes from the hole to the spot where your ball came to rest in the sand bunker. Continue to extend the line straight back from that spot and then drop your ball, with a one-stroke penalty, behind the sand bunker and on the extended line, going as far back on the course as you want.

Procedure For Relief From Interference Caused By An Immovable Obstruction-When Your Ball Is On A Putting Green (Rule 24-2): Determine the spot known as the nearest point of relief (see page 50) that is not in a sand bunker or water hazard. Lift your ball and place it, without penalty, at this nearest point of relief. Note that the nearest point of relief may be off the putting green.

Additional Pointers: (1) There is no immovable obstruction relief when your ball is in a water hazard. Instead you must proceed under the water hazard rules. (2) You are not entitled to relief from interference caused by an immovable obstruction if you have to take an unnecessarily abnormal stance or swing before there is interference, or the ball is clearly unplayable because of interference by something from which free relief is not available, such as a tree. (3) Generally, when your ball is off the putting green you are not entitled to relief from interference caused by an immovable obstruction if the obstruction simply interferes with the line of play between your ball and the hole. Note, however, that there may be a local rule that provides for relief from immovable obstructions when they are within two club-lengths of the putting green and intervene on the line of play between your ball and the hole. (4) You must use the club you intend to hit with when determining the nearest point of relief from the immovable obstruction. However, you may use any club when measuring for a club-length drop. (5) When there is a possibility that your ball might move as a result of removing a movable obstruction, mark your ball before removing the movable obstruction so you will be able to replace your ball at the proper spot, if necessary. (6) A movable water hazard stake is a movable obstruction but a movable out of bounds stake is not. Thus, if you removed an out of bounds marker you will incur a two-stroke penalty in stroke play, and the loss of the hole in match play, even if you replace it before making a stroke. (7) You will incur a two-stroke penalty in stroke play, and a loss of the hole in match play, if, when a ball is in motion, you move a movable obstruction that might influence the movement of the ball. Note, however, you may move an attended flagstick or a player's equipment.

BALL DEFLECTION

Ball Deflection Defined: If, after making a stroke, your moving ball is accidentally deflected or stopped as a result of coming in contact with someone or something other than a portion of the golf course, ball deflection has occurred. Whether or not there is relief or a penalty for ball deflection depends on the circumstances.

Ouch...what a shot! Now that's *ball deflection.*

Procedure When Your Moving Ball Hits You, Your Partner, Your Caddies Or Your Equipment (Rule 19-2):
If, after making a stroke, your moving ball is accidentally deflected or stopped by you, your partner, your caddies or equipment, you will incur a two-stroke penalty in stroke play. Play your ball where it comes to rest, unless your ball has come to rest in or on your clothes or equipment. In that case, you must lift your ball, move the article of clothing or equipment, and then drop your ball, or place it if it is on the putting green, as close as possible to where it lay, no nearer the hole. In match play, the penalty is a loss of the hole.

Procedure When Your Moving Ball Hits Your Opponent, Etc. (Rule 19-3):
If, after making a stroke in match play, your moving ball is accidentally deflected or stopped by your opponent, your opponent's caddie or their equipment, no one incurs a penalty. However, you may, at your option, play the ball where it comes to rest or replay the shot, before another stroke is made by either side, from where you last played. If you elect to play the ball from where it comes to rest and it is in or on their clothes or equipment, you may lift your ball, move the article of clothing or equipment, and then drop your ball, or place it if it is on the putting green, as close as possible to where it lay, no nearer the hole.

Procedure When Your Moving Ball Hits A Fellow-Competitor Or An Outside Agency, Etc.

(Rule 19-1): If, after making a stroke, your moving ball is accidentally deflected or stopped during stroke play by a fellow-competitor, a fellow-competitor's caddie or their equipment, or during stroke play or match play by an outside agency such as a spectator or a greenkeeper, play your ball where it comes to rest, without penalty. Exceptions: (1) If you play a stroke from off the putting green and your moving ball then comes to rest in or on a living or moving outside agency, drop a ball at the location where the contact occurred, or place it at that location if the contact occurred on the putting green. (2) If you play a stroke from the putting green and your moving ball is then deflected or stopped by, or comes to rest in or on, any living or moving outside agency, except a worm or an insect, you must cancel the stroke and replay it.

Procedure When Your Moving Ball Hits A Ball That Is In Play And At Rest (Rule 19-5):

If, after making a stroke, your moving ball is deflected or stopped as a result of hitting a ball that is in play and at rest, play your ball where it comes to rest and return the other ball to its original position. In stroke play, there is no penalty if your ball hits a ball that is in play and at rest, unless both balls are on the putting green when you make your next stroke, in which case you will incur a two-stroke penalty. In match play, there is no penalty if your ball hits your opponent's ball that is in play and at rest, even if both balls are on the putting green when you make your stroke.

Procedure When Your Moving Ball Hits Another Moving Ball (Rule 19-5): If your ball in motion after a stroke hits another ball in motion after a stroke, play your ball where it comes to rest. Exception: If your ball was put in motion after a stroke from the putting green and the other ball in motion is an outside agency, then cancel your stroke, replace your ball, and replay the stroke. You will incur a two-stroke penalty in stroke play, and the loss of the hole in match play, if the other ball was already in motion after a stroke from on the putting green when you put your ball in motion after a stroke from on the putting green, and it was not your turn to play. Otherwise, you will incur no penalty.

Additional Pointers: (1) If any player or caddie intentionally takes action to influence the position or movement of the ball, except in accordance with the rules, there is a two-stroke penalty in stroke play, and a loss of the hole in match play.

BALL MOVEMENT

Ball Movement Defined: If your ball in play has come to rest in one spot after a stroke and then moves and comes to rest in another spot before you have made another stroke, ball movement has occurred. Whether there is relief or a penalty for this ball movement depends on the circumstances.

Procedure When Your Ball Moves-General Rules (Rule 18):

1. If your ball is in play and at rest and an outside agency, such as a spectator or fellow-competitor, causes your ball to move, or if it is moved by another ball striking it, replace your ball, without penalty.

2. Unless there is a rule providing otherwise, you will incur a one-stroke penalty if your ball is in play and you, your partner or either of your caddies lift or move it, or purposely touch it (except with a club when addressing it) or if your equipment or your partner's equipment causes the ball to move. You must then replace your ball before playing your next stroke, unless the movement of the ball occurs after you have begun your stroke and you don't discontinue your stroke. (See #3 below for exceptions to this rule).

3. Replace your ball in play, without penalty, if you accidentally cause your ball to move when you are in the process of:

   a. Measuring to determine which ball is furthest from the hole.

   b. Searching for your ball lost in casual water, a burrowing animal disturbance, ground under repair, a water hazard or in a sand bunker.

   c. Repairing a hole plug or ball mark on the putting green.

   d. Removing a loose impediment when your ball is located on the putting green.

   e. Removing a movable obstruction.

   f. Marking or lifting a ball under a Rule.

   g. Placing or replacing a ball under a Rule.

Procedure When Your Ball Moves-After You Have Addressed It (Rule 18-2): When your ball is in a sand bunker or water hazard, you have addressed your ball as soon as you have taken your stance. When your ball is located outside a sand bunker of water hazard, you have addressed it as soon as you have taken your stance and grounded your club. In both stroke play and match play, if your ball in play is at rest and then moves to another spot after you address it, but before you make a stroke, you will incur a one-stroke penalty, even if you didn't do anything to cause the ball to move. You must then replace your ball before playing your next stroke, unless the movement of the ball occurs after you have begun your swing and you don't discontinue your swing.

Procedure When Your Ball Moves-After Removing Loose Impediments (Rule 18-2): If your ball is at rest, you are permitted to remove loose impediments, such as twigs and leaves, without penalty, except when both your ball and the loose impediments lie in or touch the same sand bunker or water hazard. If your ball is on the putting green and moves as a direct result of removing loose impediments, replace your ball, without penalty. If your ball is off the putting green and outside a hazard and moves to another spot as a direct result of removing loose impediments, replace your ball, with a one-stroke penalty.

Procedure When Your Ball Is Moved By Your Fellow-Competitor Or By Your Opponent (Rule 18-4): In stroke play, if your ball is in play and at rest, there is no penalty if it is touched or moved by your fellow-competitor, his caddie or equipment. Simply replace your ball. In match play, if your ball is in play and at rest and then touched or moved by your opponent, his caddie or equipment, you must replace your ball, without penalty to you. However, your opponent will incur a one-stroke penalty, unless the touching or moving of your ball by your opponent occurs when:

a. Searching for your ball; or

b. Playing a wrong ball; or

c. Measuring to determine which ball lies furthest from the hole.

Additional Pointers: (1) If you accidentally move your ball or knock it off the tee before you have played your first stroke on the hole, re-tee it, without penalty, and without counting any strokes, since your ball is not yet in play. (2) If you have made one or more strokes at your ball on the hole, your ball is in play. If your ball is in play and at rest and you accidentally touch it with your club after you address it but before making a stroke, there is no penalty as long as your ball only rocks, jiggles or oscillates and then settles back into its original position. If it does not settle back into its original position, you must replace it, with a one-stroke penalty. (3) If you fail to replace your ball when required to do so after it has moved, there is generally a two-stroke penalty in stroke play, with no additional penalty for the ball movement, and a loss of the hole in match play. (4) If your ball is at rest and is then moved by the wind or water before you address it, play it where it comes to rest in its new location, without penalty. (5) When searching for your ball, let a non-partner drive the golf cart so neither of you will be penalized for moving your ball if the cart accidentally runs over it. (6) If you address your ball on the putting green and then step away from it, you will be penalized for ball movement if it thereafter moves, even if you haven't re-addressed the ball. To avoid this penalty when you feel the ball is precariously balanced, mark and lift the ball. If it then moves after being replaced but before it is addressed again, there is no penalty since it was not address after being lifted and taken out of play. (7) If, after a stroke, your ball is accidentally stopped by you, your partner, or either of your caddies or equipment, you will incur a two-stroke penalty in stroke play, and a loss of the hole in match play.

Procedure For Lifting And Replacing A Ball (Rule 20-1 & 20-3): When your ball is to be lifted under the rules, it may be lifted by you or anyone you authorize. When an authorized person lifts your ball, you are responsible for any breach of the rules. When your ball must be replaced, it need not be replaced by the person who marked and lifted it. However, it may only be replaced by you, your partner, or the person who lifted it. When a ball must be replaced, always mark its position before lifting it, or you will incur a one-stroke penalty.

Procedure For Lifting A Ball Which Is Off The Putting Green-To Determine Its Fitness Or Identity (Rule 5-3 & 12-2): You may lift your ball at any time to see if it is unfit for play. Your ball is considered unfit for play, and may be replaced by another ball, if it is visibly cut, cracked or out of shape, but not if it is just scuffed or marred. You may also lift what you think is your ball at any time to identify it, except when it is in a sand bunker or water hazard. Before lifting your ball when it's off the putting green, make sure you advise a fellow-competitor or marker in stroke play, or an opponent in match play, of your intention to lift it, give them an opportunity to watch, and then mark your ball before touching or lifting it. You are not permitted to clean your ball more than is necessary to identify it, or at all to check its fitness. If you fail to follow any of the steps of this procedure for lifting your ball, you will incur a one-stroke penalty.

<u>Procedure For Lifting A Ball Which Is Off The Putting Green To Prevent It From Assisting Or Interfering With Play (Rule 22)</u>: Except when another ball is in motion, you may (1) have another player's ball lifted if you think that the other player's ball might interfere, either physically or mentally, with your play or assist the play of one of the other players, or (2) mark and lift your own ball if you think it might assist any other player. Note, however, that unless requested to do so by another player, you are not entitled to mark and lift your own ball when it is at rest off the putting green simply because you think it might interfere with the play of another player. In stroke play, but not in match play, if you are asked to lift your assisting or interfering ball, you may play first rather than lift your ball. You will incur a one-stroke penalty in both stroke play and match play if you clean your assisting or interfering ball, except when it is lifted from the putting green.

DROPPING YOUR BALL

Dropping Your Ball Defined: Under certain circumstances you will be required to put your ball in play by dropping it within a certain area or by dropping it at a specific spot.

Wait, John.
You have to *stand erect*
before dropping your ball!

Procedure For How To Drop Your Ball (Rule 20-2): To properly drop your ball, you are required to stand erect, hold your ball at shoulder height and arm's length, and then release it. You may hold the ball in front of you or to your side at the time of the drop. You will incur a one-stroke penalty in both stroke play and match play if you play a ball that has been dropped in an incorrect manner. When dropped, the ball must first strike a part of the course where it is required to be dropped or it must be re-dropped. If the ball touches you or your equipment during the drop, you must re-drop it, without penalty, until it is dropped correctly.

Procedure For Where To Drop Your Ball (Rule 20-2): When you are required to drop your ball as close to a specific spot as possible, your ball must strike a part of the course no nearer the hole than that specific spot. However, if you don't know the exact location of the spot, you may estimate its location. If you are required to drop your ball in a sand bunker or water hazard, it must be dropped in, and come to rest in, the sand bunker or water hazard. Refer to the section which deals with your particular situation when determining where to drop your ball.

Procedure For When To Re-drop Your Ball (Rule 20-2): You must re-drop your ball, without penalty, if you drop your ball and it rolls:

    1. And comes to rest out of bounds.

    2. Into and comes to rest in a sand bunker or water hazard.

3. Out of and comes to rest outside a sand bunker or water hazard.

4. Onto and comes to rest on a putting green.

5. And comes to rest more than two club-lengths from where it first strikes a part of the course.

6. And comes to rest closer to the hole than its original position or closer to the hole than the position you estimated, unless otherwise permitted by the rules.

7. And comes to rest closer to the hole than the spot where your original ball last crossed the margin of the water hazard when you are taking water hazard relief.

8. And comes to rest closer to the hole than the spot where your original ball last crossed the margin of the casual water, ground under repair, immovable obstruction, or burrowing animal disturbance when it became lost.

9. Back into and comes to rest in the embedded ball pitch-mark from which you lifted it or back into interference caused by casual water, ground under repair, an immovable obstruction, or a burrowing animal disturbance when your lift was from the same condition.

Procedure For Where And How To Re-Drop Your Ball (Rule 20-2): When you are required to re-drop your ball, you must re-drop it at the same location where it was required to be dropped the first time. If, after a re-drop, the ball again rolls into any of the places mentioned in 1 through 9, do not drop the ball a third time. Instead, place the ball as close as possible to the spot where the ball first struck a part of the course when it was re-dropped.

Additional Pointers: (1) If you drop or place your ball in the wrong location but have not yet played a stroke at it from that location, re-drop it in the correct location, without penalty. (2) If you play a stroke at your ball in play that has been dropped or placed at the wrong location, or has not been re-dropped when required, or replaced when required, you will incur a two-stroke penalty in stroke play, if you have not committed *a serious breach* as determined by the committee, and the loss of the hole in match play. (3) You may use any club to measure the one or two club-length distance within which to drop your ball.   However, you must then use the same club when determining whether your ball has rolled more than two club-lengths away from where it first struck a part of the course. (4) No one else may drop your ball for you. (5) When your ball in play has been lifted, it is again in play as soon as you drop or place it. (6) If you substitute a ball for your ball in play, your substituted ball is in play as soon as you drop or place it.

PLAYING THE WRONG BALL

Playing The Wrong Ball Defined: You have played a wrong ball when you have played a stroke at any ball other than (1) your ball in play, (2) your provisional ball, (3) your second ball, in stroke play, that is being played because you're unsure of your rights, or (4) your second ball, in stroke play, that is being played because your original ball was played from the wrong place. A wrong ball includes another player's ball, an abandoned ball, and your own ball when it is no longer in play.

Procedure When You Play A Wrong Ball- From Outside A Sand Bunker Or Outside A Water Hazard (Rule 15): In stroke play, you will incur a two-stroke penalty if you play a wrong ball from outside a hazard. Strokes played with the wrong ball are not counted. Thus, if you play three strokes with your original ball before playing the wrong ball, you will be hitting six with your original ball when you discover your mistake, regardless of the number of strokes taken with the wrong ball. Once you discover that you're playing the wrong ball you must correct your mistake by returning to the location of your original ball and completing the hole with it. If you make a stroke on the next hole before correcting your mistake, or if you leave the putting green on the final hole before declaring your intention to correct the mistake made on the final hole, you will be disqualified. In match play, the first player to play a wrong ball from outside a hazard loses the hole. If both you and your opponent play wrong balls, and it can't be determined who was the first to do so, continue playing the hole with the wrong balls, without penalty.

Procedure When You Play A Wrong Ball- From A Sand Bunker Or From A Water Hazard (Rule 15): There is no penalty, and you don't count any strokes taken, when you play a wrong ball from a

sand bunker or from a water hazard. Simply replace the wrong ball in its original position and lie in the sand bunker or water hazard and then continue play using your correct ball.

Additional Pointers: (1) Always put an identifying mark on your ball so you won't accidentally hit another player's ball. (2) If your first stroke from the teeing ground is played with a ball that belongs to someone else and you finish the hole with it, you have not played a wrong ball since a ball played from the teeing ground into the hole is not a wrong ball, even if it does not belong to you. (3) You are required to play the same ball from the teeing ground into the hole unless a rule permits you to substitute a ball for your original ball. (4) If you substitute one of your balls for your original ball during the play of a hole when there is no rule permitting such a substitution, the substituted ball is not a wrong ball but instead becomes your ball in play as soon as you place or drop it. If you then play a stroke at this substituted ball before correcting your error, you will incur a two-stroke penalty in stroke play and a loss of the hole in match play, but no penalty for hitting a wrong ball.

SEARCHING FOR YOUR BALL

Searching For Your Ball Defined: When you hit your ball and can't find it, you are allowed to search for it for a maximum of five minutes before it becomes a lost ball.

Procedure For Searching For Your Ball-Outside A Sand Bunker And Outside A Water Hazard (Rule 12-1): When searching for your ball outside a sand bunker or water hazard, you may touch or bend long grass, bushes and other vegetation, but only to the extent necessary to find and identify your ball. If you, your partner, or your caddies cause your ball to move during the search, you must replace it and take a one-stroke penalty, unless the ball is in a sand bunker, a water hazard, casual water, ground under repair or a burrowing animal disturbance. In addition, if you improve your lie, your line of play, or the area of your intended swing during your search activity, you will incur a two-stroke penalty in stroke play, and a loss of the hole in match play.

Procedure For Searching For Your Ball-In A Sand Bunker Or Water Hazard (Rule 12-1):

When searching for your ball in a sand bunker or water hazard, you may remove sand and loose impediments by using your hand, your club, a rake or various other means. If your ball moves during your search, simply replace it before playing, without penalty. Since there is no penalty for playing a wrong ball from a sand bunker or water hazard, you should remove only enough sand or enough loose impediments to see a portion of a ball. You are not permitted to lift the ball in order to identify it as your own ball. If you remove an excess of material, there is no penalty as long as you re-cover the ball so only a portion of it is visible. If, after hitting out of the sand bunker or water hazard, you discover that the ball you played is not your own, replace it, without penalty, and don't count any strokes played with it from the hazard. Then proceed to look for your ball.

Additional Pointers: (1) If you accidentally move your ball during your search for it when it is in water in a water hazard, or during your search for it when it is in casual water, ground under repair or in a burrowing animal disturbance, there is no penalty. Simply replace it or proceed with the other options of play that are available in those situations.

CLEANING YOUR BALL

Procedure For Cleaning Your Ball (Rule 21): You will incur a one-stroke penalty if you clean your ball when it is not permitted. When your ball is at rest, you are permitted to mark, lift, and then clean your ball as follows:

1. *On the putting green:* You may clean your ball, without penalty.

2. *Off the putting green:* You may clean your ball, without penalty, when the rules permit you to lift your ball. Exceptions:

a. When you lift your ball to identify it, you may clean it, but only to the extent necessary to identify it.

b. When you lift your ball to determine its fitness for play or when you lift it to prevent it from assisting or interfering with play, you may not clean it.

Additional Pointers: (1) Although not recommended, when you are permitted to clean your ball, you may do so by rubbing it on the putting green, as long as such rubbing is not done for the purpose of testing the surface of the putting green.

THE PUTTING GREEN

On The Putting Green Defined: The putting green is that part of the course that is specially prepared for putting. It does not include the short grass around it that is often called the apron, the fringe or the collar. A ball is on the putting green when any part of the ball touches the putting green.

Procedures Regarding The Line Of Putt (Rule 16-1): It is a two-stroke penalty in stroke play, and a loss of the hole in match play, to:

1. Press anything down when removing loose impediments or movable obstructions on your line of putt. You are now permitted to remove loose impediments on the putting green by using any means, such as a towel or your glove, as long as you don't press anything down when doing so.

2. Repair irregularities on your line of putt, including raised tufts of grass or spike marks. Exception: You may repair any damage on your line of putt that has been caused by the impact of a ball or by the plugging of a former hole, even if your ball is not yet on the surface of the putting green.

3. Allow your partner or your caddies to stand on or close to an extension of the line of putt, behind the ball, while you are putting.

4. Roll a ball on the putting green, during play, to test the surface or determine the break of a putt.

5. Brush aside dew that is on your line of putt since dew is not casual water or a loose impediment.

6. Allow your partner or your caddies to touch your line of putt in order to indicate your line of putt.

7. Putt from the wrong location. If you move your ball-marker one or more clubhead-lengths so it will not interfere with the play, stance or stroke of another player, make sure to return the ball-marker to its original position before replacing and then putting your ball or you will be putting from the wrong location.

8. Putt croquet style, where one leg is on each side of the line of putt, or putt with either foot touching the line of putt or an extension of the line behind the ball.

Procedure Regarding The Flagstick (Rule 17): It is a two-stroke penalty in stroke play, and the loss of the hole in match play, to:

1. Strike an unattended flagstick with your ball, when you play a stroke from the putting green.

2. Strike an attended flagstick or the authorized person attending it, with your ball, when you play a stroke from on or off the putting green.

3. Authorize the removal of an unattended flagstick while your ball is moving.

Procedure When Your Ball Is Overhanging The Hole (Rule 16-2): If any part of your ball is hanging over the lip of the cup, you are given enough time to reach the hole without unreasonable delay. You then have ten seconds to determine if your ball is at rest. If your ball falls into the hole before the ten-second period has expired, there is no extra stroke. If your ball falls into the hole after the ten-second period has expired, add one stroke to your score.

You have 10 seconds!

Please fall in!

Procedure When Your Ball Is On The Wrong Putting Green (Rule 25-3): If your ball comes to rest on a putting green of a hole other than the one you're playing, including a practice green on the course, you must lift and drop your ball within one club-length of and not nearer the hole than the nearest point of relief that is not in a hazard or on a putting green. When dropped, your ball must first strike a part of the course that is outside a hazard and off the putting green. If your ball lies off the putting green, there is no relief under this rule, even though the wrong putting green may interfere with your stance or the area of your intended swing.

Procedure When You Fail To Hole Out (Rule 3-2): In stroke play competition, if you fail to hole out on any hole, you will be disqualified unless you correct your mistake before playing a stroke on the next hole, or, if it's the last hole, before you leave the putting green of the last hole.

Additional Pointers: (1) When your ball is at rest on the putting green, you may mark, lift and clean it. (2) When your ball is in play, if you accidentally hit it with your putter and it moves and comes to rest in another location, you must replace the ball and take a one-stroke penalty. (3) If your clubs and an unattended flagstick are lying on the putting green, you are permitted to move your clubs out of the path of a moving ball, but not the flagstick. (4) If the hole is between you and your ball and you reach across the hole to tap your ball in, there is no penalty for standing astride or on your line of putt because the line of putt does not extend beyond the hole.

ADVICE

Advice Defined: Advice is defined as any counsel or suggestion that could influence you in determining (1) your play, (2) the choice of a club, or (3) the method of making a stroke.

Procedure For Asking For, Or Giving, Advice (Rule 8): You will incur a two-stroke penalty in stroke play, and a loss of the hole in match play, if you ask for advice from anyone except your partners or your caddies, or if you give advice to anyone other

than your partner, during a round. Some examples of what is permitted and what is not permitted during a round are as follows:

1. You are not permitted to give advice to, or receive advice from, anyone other than your partner or your caddies about how to swing a club or what club to use for a specific shot.

2. You are permitted to ask anyone questions, or answer questions, about the rules of golf.

3. You are permitted to ask or answer questions about matters of public information such as the position of the flagstick on the putting green or the distance from a permanent object, such as a tree, to the middle of the putting green. However, you are not permitted to ask anyone, other than your partner or your caddies, about the distance from a non-permanent object, such as your own ball, to another object.

4. When your ball is off the putting green, anyone may indicated the line of play to you, but no one may stand on or close to the line, or an extension of the line beyond the hole, or leave any indicator on it while you are playing the stroke, except the flagstick may be held up at the hole.

FOUR-BALL COMPETITIONS

Four-Ball Competition Defined: In four-ball stroke play and four-ball match play, players form two person teams. Each player plays his own ball on each hole. The lower score of the two partners is the team's score for the hole.

Procedure To Determine When Partners Are Penalized During Four-Ball Competitions (Rule 30 & 31): In a four-ball competition, your partner will not be penalized when you incur a penalty for the breach of a rule, unless your breach assists your partner. In four-ball match play, if you breach a rule and it adversely affects an opponent's play, both you and your partner will be penalized.

Additional Pointers: (1) When it's your turn to play, your partner may play first, even though your partner's ball may be closer to the hole than your ball or any other player's ball. (2) If you carry more than fourteen clubs, both you and your partner will be penalized. (3) In four ball stroke play, if you play a stroke with a wrong ball, other than from a sand bunker or water hazard, you will incur a two-stroke penalty and must then play the correct ball. In four ball match play, if you play a stroke with a wrong ball, you will be disqualified from further play of the hole. Your partner will not be penalized when you play a wrong ball, even if the wrong ball you played belongs to your partner. (4) You may represent your side for all or any part of a competition. Your absent partner may join the competition at any time between holes, but may not join the competition during play of a hole. (5) In match play, but not stroke play, you or your opponent may concede a stroke, a hole, or the match. The concession, once given, cannot be declined or withdrawn. (6) In match play, you may continue to complete play of the hole even if you your next stroke has been conceded or you have been disqualified from the hole for breach of a rule. However, if your continued play assists your partner in a four-ball or best-ball match, your partner will be disqualified for the hole. For example, if your putt is conceded but you want to putt out anyway, wait until everyone has completed the hole so a claim cannot be made that your putt assisted your partner's play.

PRACTICING ON THE COURSE

Procedure For Practicing On The Course-Before The Start Of A Competition (Rule 7-1): On the day of a stoke play competition or play-off, you will be disqualified if you practice on the course or test the surface of any putting green on the course before starting play. Exception: You may practice chipping or putting on or near the first teeing ground. When two or more rounds of a stroke play competition are to be played over consecutive days, you are prohibited from practicing on the course between rounds. On the day of a match play competition, you may practice anywhere on the course before the start of the match, unless prohibited by local rule.

Procedure For Practicing On The Course-During A Round (Rule 7-2): You will incur a two-stroke penalty in stroke play, and the loss of the hole in match play, if you play a practice stroke on the course during the play of a hole or between the play of two holes. Exception: You may practice putting or chipping on or near the putting green of the hole last played, any practice putting green, or on the teeing ground of the next hole to be played, but not from a sand bunker or water hazard and not if it unduly delays play.

Additional Pointers: (1) A practice *swing* is not a practice *stroke* and may be taken at any time, without penalty, as long as you don't otherwise breach the rules. (2) If you are penalized for practicing on the course between the play of two holes, the penalty applies to the next hole rather than the one you just played. (3) In match play, you may finish playing a hole even though the result of the hole has been decided. Strokes played under such circumstances are not deemed to be practice strokes. (4) The committee may allow practice on the course or part of the course on any day or between rounds of a stroke play competition. (5) The committee may prohibit practice on the course or part of the course on any day of a match play competition. (6) You will not be penalized for practicing during play if you casually flick a range ball with a club when trying to keep the course in proper order.

STAKED TREES

Procedure For Relief From A Staked Tree When No Local Rule For Relief Has Been Adopted: To prevent damage to young trees, they are often staked or otherwise identified. A *stake* supporting a tree is usually deemed an immovable obstruction and you are thus entitled to immovable obstruction relief from the stake. However, unless there is a local rule to the contrary, you are not entitled to immovable obstruction relief from the entire tree as well.

Procedure For Relief From A Staked Tree Where Local Rules For Relief Have Been Adopted (App. 1): Typically, local rules provide that if a staked tree interferes with your stance or the area of your intended swing, you may drop your ball, without penalty, within one club-length of the nearest point of relief, no nearer the hole and not in a water hazard, a sand bunker or on a putting green. Note that the nearest point of relief is the closest spot, no nearer the hole, where you can take your stance without the tree interfering with your ball, feet, or swing. This nearest point may result in the tree being directly between your ball and the target. There is no relief if the staked tree only interferes with your line of play.

STRIKING THE BALL MORE THAN ONCE

Procedure When You Strike The Ball More Than Once (Rule 14-4): If your club strikes the ball two or more times while making one stroke, count it as two strokes in total, one stroke for the swing at the ball plus one penalty stroke.

MOVING YOUR BALL-MARKER

Procedure For Moving Your Ball-Marker When It Interferes With The Play, Stance, Or Stroke Of Another Player (Rule 20-1): If a rule requires you to replace your ball when you lift it, the position of your ball must be marked before you lift it. If your ball-marker then interferes with the play, stance, or stroke of another player, you should place your ball-marker one or more clubhead-lengths to one side to eliminate the interference. Remember to return your ball-marker to its former position before replacing your ball and playing your next stroke, or you will incur a two-stoke penalty in stroke play, and a loss of the hole in match play, for playing your ball from the wrong location.

WINTER RULES

Procedure When Playing By Winter Rules (App.1): When adverse weather affects the playing conditions of a course, local winter rules may permit you to move your ball to preferred lies. Since winter rules differ from course to course, they should be in writing and posted. Often, winter rules provide that a ball at rest on the fairway may be lifted, cleaned and then placed, without penalty. The ball must usually be placed within one club-length, no nearer the hole, at a location which duplicates as nearly as possible the stance required to be played by the original lie. Before playing a course where winter rules are in effect, determine:

1. If the lie of your ball may be improved in the fairway only;

2. If your ball may be cleaned when lifted; and

3. The distance your ball may be moved from its original location at rest.

GLOSSARY

Addressing The Ball: When your ball is outside a sand bunker or water hazard, you have addressed the ball when you have taken a stance and ground your club behind the ball. When your ball is in a sand bunker or water hazard, you are not permitted to ground your club, and thus, you have addressed the ball as soon as you have taken a stance.

Ball In Play: Your ball is in play as soon as you make a stroke from the teeing ground. Your ball continues to be in play until it is holed out unless it is: (1) lost, (2) out of bounds, (3) lifted, or (4) replaced by another ball which has been substituted for it, even if there is no rule permitting the substitution. If your original ball or substituted ball in play has been lifted, it is again in play when dropped or placed.

Competitor: Anyone playing in a stroke play competition is a competitor.

Fellow-Competitor: Anyone playing in a stroke play competition, in your same group, is your fellow-competitor.

Four-Ball Competition: In four-ball stroke play and four-ball match play, two players act as a team and play their better ball against the better ball of another team of two players.

Line Of Play: Your line of play is the direction you want your ball to travel after a stroke. It includes a reasonable distance on each side of the intended direction, extends vertically upwards from the ground, but does not go beyond the hole.

Line Of Putt: Your line of putt is the direction you want your ball to travel on the putting green after a stroke. It includes a reasonable distance on each side of the intended direction, but it does not go beyond the hole.

Margin: The margin is a real or imagined line that defines an area of the course, such as a water hazard or ground under repair.

Marker: A marker records the score of a competitor in a stroke play competition. The marker is often a fellow-competitor.

Match Play: Match play is a competition based on the number of holes won, rather than the strokes played.

Opponent: The person or side you are competing against in match play is your opponent.

Outside Agency: An outside agency is a person or thing that is not part of the match in match play, and a person or thing that is not part of the competitor's side in stroke play. Examples of outside agencies include animals, birds, inanimate objects, referees, markers and spectators. Wind and water are not outside agencies.

Provisional Ball: A provisional ball is a ball that is played in order to save time when there is a reasonable possibility that your original ball is out of bounds or is lost outside a water hazard.

Rub Of The Green: A rub of the green occurs when your ball in motion is accidentally deflected or stopped by an outside agency.

Second Ball: In stroke play, if a competitor is uncertain about the proper way to proceed in a situation, a second ball may be played on the hole in addition to the ball in play. Thereafter, a ruling must be obtained to determine which of the two balls was played pursuant to the rules.

Stroke: A stroke occurs when you make a forward movement of your club with the intention of fairly striking at and moving the ball. If you intentionally stop your downswing before the clubhead reaches your ball, you have not made a stroke.

Stroke Play: Stroke play is a competition based on the total number of strokes played, rather than the number of holes won. Stroke play is also known as medal play.

Substituted Ball: A substituted ball is a ball that you put into play for your original ball that was either in play, lost, out of bounds, or lifted.

Taking A Stance: You have taken a stance when you have placed your feet in position in preparation for making a stroke.

Through The Green: Through the green is the entire area of the golf course except for all the sand bunkers on the course, all the water hazards on the course, the teeing ground of the hole being played, and the putting green of the hole being played.

INDEX

NOTES